THE HIDDEN TREASURE INSIDE

A Modern Adventurer's Guide to Solving Hidden Riches Inspired By Jon Collins-Black

Ben Mario

TABLE OF CONTENTS

Introduction: The Modern Treasure Hunt Phenomenon

Overview of Jon Collins-Black's Treasure Hunt

In recent years, the phenomenon of real-world treasure hunts has captivated the imaginations of people across the globe. With the rise of social media and online communities, individuals have been drawn to the idea of solving complex puzzles, following cryptic clues, and seeking out hidden treasures in real life. One of the most exciting recent examples of this trend is Jon Collins-Black's multi-million-dollar treasure hunt. Collins-Black, an entrepreneur, author, and fantasy enthusiast, has hidden five treasure chests across the United States, each one containing rare artifacts, gold, and other valuable collectibles worth over $2 million in total.

The chests, each a puzzle box in itself, are scattered in secret locations and come with a unique twist: the clues to find them are hidden within Collins-Black's book, *There's Treasure Inside.* In this book, Collins-Black offers hints and riddles that, when deciphered correctly, point the reader to the location of one of the five treasure troves. But the hunt isn't meant to be a simple scavenger chase; Collins-Black has designed it to challenge participants, requiring them to think creatively, collaborate with others, and take into account elements of history, geography, and culture.

Collins-Black's treasure hunt is not the first of its kind. Inspired by a long lineage of real-life treasure hunts, including the infamous Forrest Fenn's buried treasure in the Rocky Mountains, Collins-Black saw an opportunity to provide a more accessible adventure, spreading the chests across different parts of the country. This dispersion ensures that more people, regardless of their location, can participate and feel that they have a real chance at uncovering one of the hidden fortunes.

The five chests, according to Collins-Black, contain a vast assortment of collectibles, including gold, rare Pokémon cards, shipwreck bounty, sports memorabilia, and items with significant historical value. For example, one chest contains a brooch once owned by former First Lady Jacqueline Kennedy Onassis, while others hold objects linked to figures like Pablo Picasso and Wilma Rudolph. Collins-Black has made it clear that these treasures were not randomly selected but carefully curated to create a once-in-a-lifetime experience for those who seek them.

While the specifics of the clues remain secret within *There's Treasure Inside*, the treasure hunt has already sparked widespread interest, with online forums and communities buzzing with activity. Thousands of participants have gathered on platforms like Discord and Reddit, sharing theories, exchanging ideas, and working together to crack the codes. The treasure hunt has captured the imagination of many who are drawn to the challenge of solving the puzzles and the allure of discovering something valuable in real life.

The Inspiration Behind the Hunt

Jon Collins-Black's treasure hunt did not emerge from a vacuum. It draws inspiration from various sources, both historical and personal, that shaped his vision of an adventure that blends intellectual challenge with physical exploration. One of the most prominent influences was Forrest Fenn, an art dealer and adventurer who, in 2010, hid a treasure chest filled with gold and jewels somewhere in the Rocky Mountains. Fenn's treasure hunt captivated the world, leading to the search lasting nearly a decade before the chest was discovered in 2020. The sense of mystery, the chase, and the thrill of the unknown inspired many, including Collins-Black.

However, Collins-Black envisioned something different from Fenn's singular, static treasure chest. While Fenn's hunt was exhilarating, it was geographically limited to the Rocky Mountains, leaving many people across the country unable to participate without traveling long distances. Collins-Black sought to create a more democratic hunt, one that spread the chests across multiple states, making them more accessible to a wider audience. His treasure hunt taps into the spirit of adventure and discovery that lies at the heart of many childhood fantasies, especially for those who grew up reading books about hidden treasure or playing games like *Dungeons & Dragons*.

In interviews, Collins-Black has spoken about his lifelong love of fantasy, mythology, and storytelling. He grew up immersed in the world of fantastical tales, which eventually led him to careers in both music and writing. This creative background gave him the tools to design a hunt that's not only about finding physical treasure but also about engaging with a narrative that he has built around the chests. Each puzzle, clue, and riddle is crafted with the intent of making the treasure hunter think deeply and reflect on the journey, much like a player in a role-playing game who uncovers parts of a story as they advance through the adventure.

Moreover, Collins-Black's treasure hunt is designed to bring people together. He encourages collaboration and collective problem-solving, knowing that the complexity of the clues often requires more than one perspective. Many treasure hunters have formed online communities to pool their knowledge and brainstorm solutions to the puzzles, creating a shared experience that is as much about the social interaction as it is about the search. This collaborative spirit was central to Collins-Black's vision for the hunt, reflecting his belief that real-world adventure can bring people closer and foster a sense of connection across distances.

Why This Book? Helping You Decode the Clues Faster

While Jon Collins-Black's book, *There's Treasure Inside*, is the official guide to the treasure hunt, this book aims to assist treasure seekers by providing additional strategies, insights, and methods that can help decode the clues more efficiently. The goal of this book is not to replicate or compete with *There's Treasure Inside* but to complement it by offering readers a deeper understanding of the broader puzzle-solving strategies and tools that can be applied to a treasure hunt of this scale.

For those who are serious about finding one of Collins-Black's treasure chests, this book serves as a guide to fast-track their progress. Rather than focusing on the exact clues in *There's Treasure Inside*—which, of course, remain exclusive to that book—this guide delves into the types of puzzles Collins-Black is likely to use, the patterns in treasure hunts, and the best practices for interpreting cryptic hints. By exploring common puzzle structures, historical references, and treasure-hunting tactics, this book equips readers with the skills to decode clues faster and more effectively.

One of the key reasons for this book's existence is to bridge the gap between casual readers and serious treasure hunters. While *There's Treasure Inside* is designed to be enjoyed by anyone, even those who have no intention of embarking on the hunt, this book is for those who are committed to the chase. It provides insights into how treasure hunts typically work, explains the logic behind Collins-Black's puzzle construction, and gives practical advice on how to approach each step of the journey.

For example, Collins-Black's background in storytelling and role-playing games suggests that many of his clues are likely to be narrative-driven. Understanding the underlying story within *There's Treasure Inside*—the fictional narrative that may link the chests together—can offer valuable insights into the locations of the treasure. Furthermore, Collins-Black's use of historical and cultural artifacts points to the importance of research. Treasure hunters who have a strong grasp of American history, art, and literature may find themselves better equipped to solve certain puzzles.

Finally, this book emphasizes the importance of collaboration. One of the unique features of Collins-Black's treasure hunt is the way it has brought people together, both online and offline. This book offers advice on how to effectively collaborate with other treasure hunters, share information without giving away too much, and use collective intelligence to crack the toughest clues. By leveraging the power of community, treasure hunters can significantly increase their chances of success.

Jon Collins-Black's treasure hunt represents a modern take on a timeless adventure. This book serves as a resource for those who want to dive deeper into the hunt and increase their chances of finding one of the hidden chests. Through a combination of strategy, research, and collaboration, readers can turn the clues in *There's Treasure Inside* into actionable leads that bring them closer to discovering treasure worth over $2 million.

Chapter 1: Understanding Collins-Black's Method

Jon Collins-Black's treasure hunt has captured the imagination of adventurers and puzzle solvers across the United States. With five chests hidden in secret locations, each containing rare and valuable artifacts, Collins-Black has designed a treasure hunt that is both thrilling and challenging. For those who are serious about uncovering one of these hidden treasures, understanding Collins-Black's method is key. In this chapter, we will explore what we know about the chests, analyze the key themes from his works, and delve into the puzzle design insights that his background reveals.

What We Know About the Chests

Collins-Black's treasure chests are no ordinary containers of gold and jewels. Each one is a carefully crafted puzzle box filled with a collection of rare and valuable items, including collectibles, gold, and historical artifacts. The total value of the five chests exceeds $2 million, with some chests being more valuable than others.

One of the defining characteristics of Collins-Black's treasure hunt is the diversity of the items contained in the chests. From rare Pokémon cards and shipwreck treasures to sports memorabilia and gold, the contents of the chests reflect Collins-Black's eclectic taste and deep appreciation for history and culture. Some of the most notable items hidden in the chests include a brooch once owned by Jacqueline Kennedy Onassis, a 96-carat emerald, and Wilma Rudolph's 1960 Olympic gold medal. These treasures are not only valuable in monetary terms but also carry significant historical and emotional weight, making the discovery of any chest a once-in-a-lifetime experience.

Collins-Black's treasure chests are distributed across the United States, with each one hidden in a location that can be uncovered through clues provided in his book, *There's Treasure Inside*. The locations are diverse, ensuring that participants from different parts of the country have an equal chance of discovering one of the chests. Collins-Black has stated that no chest is buried, nor does finding a chest require any dangerous activities like diving or climbing.

Instead, the treasure hunters must use their wits to interpret the clues and pinpoint the location of each chest.

The treasure hunt's accessibility is a major factor in its widespread appeal. Unlike many other treasure hunts, which may involve remote or difficult-to-reach locations, Collins-Black has designed his hunt to be approachable for people of average health and ability. This inclusivity ensures that the treasure hunt is open to a wide audience, from families looking for a fun adventure to serious puzzle solvers aiming to crack the code.

Analyzing the Key Themes from His Works

Understanding Jon Collins-Black's method for hiding his treasure requires a close examination of the themes present in his works. Collins-Black is not just a treasure hunter; he is also an author, musician, and fantasy enthusiast with a deep love for storytelling. His background in creative writing and his passion for fantasy narratives play a significant role in shaping the treasure hunt and the clues he has created.

One of the key themes that emerges from Collins-Black's work is the idea of adventure as a journey of self-discovery. Much like the heroes in fantasy novels and role-playing games, treasure hunters in Collins-Black's world are encouraged to explore both the external world and their own inner landscape. The puzzles and clues are designed to challenge not just the intellect but also the imagination, requiring participants to think creatively and approach problems from different perspectives.

Another important theme is collaboration. Collins-Black's treasure hunt encourages teamwork and collective problem-solving, much like the dynamics of a group of adventurers working together to solve a mystery in a fantasy world. In interviews, Collins-Black has emphasized the importance of collaboration in cracking the codes. Many treasure hunters have taken this to heart, forming online communities and discussion groups where they share theories, exchange ideas, and work together to solve the puzzles.

The use of historical and cultural references is another recurring theme in Collins-Black's works. The items hidden in the treasure chests are not just valuable in terms of their monetary worth but also in terms of their historical significance. By including artifacts linked to figures like George Washington, Amelia Earhart, and Pablo Picasso, Collins-Black has created a treasure hunt that is as much about learning and discovery as it is about the thrill of finding a chest. The historical context of these items often provides important clues to the location of the chests, making knowledge of history and culture an essential tool for treasure hunters.

In addition to history, geography plays a crucial role in Collins-Black's treasure hunt. The clues in *There's Treasure Inside* often reference specific landmarks, natural features, or historical sites, requiring treasure hunters to have a deep understanding of the geography of the United States. Collins-Black has stated that the treasure is hidden in locations that are publicly accessible and do not require any trespassing, meaning that participants will need to carefully study maps and learn about the history of various regions to uncover the treasure.

Finally, Collins-Black's works often emphasize the idea of puzzles as metaphors for life's challenges. In this sense, the treasure hunt is not just about finding gold or rare artifacts—it is about the process of solving the puzzle itself. Collins-Black wants treasure hunters to enjoy the journey and to see the hunt as a test of their problem-solving abilities, perseverance, and creativity.

Puzzle Design Insights: What Collins-Black's Background Reveals

Jon Collins-Black's background in writing, music, and fantasy gaming has a profound influence on the way he designs his puzzles. For those looking to solve the clues in *There's Treasure Inside*, understanding his approach to puzzle design is essential.

Collins-Black's early fascination with games like *Dungeons & Dragons* provides a key insight into his puzzle design philosophy. In role-playing games (RPGs), players are often presented with complex, multi-layered puzzles that require both logical thinking and creative problem-solving. Collins-Black's treasure hunt is similar in that the clues are not straightforward riddles but rather intricate puzzles that require participants to think outside the box. The clues often have multiple layers of meaning, and solving them requires a combination of knowledge, intuition, and collaboration.

In *There's Treasure Inside*, the clues are not presented in isolation but are woven into the narrative of the book. This narrative-driven approach to puzzle design is a hallmark of

Collins-Black's style. He has crafted a story around the treasure hunt, with each chapter offering hints that are embedded within the broader context of the narrative. This means that participants must not only solve the individual puzzles but also understand how the story as a whole relates to the location of the treasure. Collins-Black's experience as a storyteller shines through in this aspect of the treasure hunt, making the clues more engaging and challenging than a typical riddle.

One of the key elements of Collins-Black's puzzle design is the use of symbolic and visual clues. Many treasure hunters have noted that some of the clues in *There's Treasure Inside* seem to be based on visual patterns or symbols that require careful observation and interpretation. This reliance on visual clues is consistent with Collins-Black's background in music and art, where symbols and patterns often play a crucial role in conveying meaning. Treasure hunters who are adept at recognizing patterns and interpreting visual information may find themselves at an advantage when solving Collins-Black's puzzles.

Another important aspect of Collins-Black's puzzle design is his use of ciphers and codes. In interviews, Collins-Black has hinted that some of the clues in *There's Treasure Inside* may involve cryptographic elements, requiring treasure hunters to decipher hidden messages or break codes. This is a common technique in puzzle design, particularly in treasure hunts, where participants must uncover hidden information by translating coded messages. Collins-Black's interest in puzzles and cryptography suggests that treasure hunters will need to familiarize themselves with various forms of codebreaking in order to unlock the secrets of the treasure's location.

Collins-Black's background in fantasy gaming also suggests that his puzzles may require participants to think about the world in non-literal terms. In fantasy games, puzzles often involve magical or supernatural elements that defy the logic of the real world. While Collins-Black's treasure hunt is firmly rooted in reality, his clues may require treasure hunters to think metaphorically or abstractly. This means that participants should be prepared to interpret the clues in ways that go beyond their surface meaning, considering how the story and the treasure might be connected to larger themes or ideas.

Finally, Collins-Black's treasure hunt is designed to reward persistence and perseverance. Much like the heroes in fantasy novels or role-playing games, treasure hunters in Collins-Black's world must be prepared to face setbacks and challenges along the way. The clues are intentionally difficult, requiring multiple steps to solve, and Collins-Black has stated that he expects the treasure hunt to take some time. However, for those who are willing to put in the effort and work collaboratively with others, the rewards are immense.

In conclusion, understanding Jon Collins-Black's method is crucial for anyone who wants to succeed in his treasure hunt. By examining the key themes in his works and analyzing his approach to puzzle design, treasure hunters can gain valuable insights into how to interpret the clues and uncover one of the hidden chests. Collins-Black's treasure hunt is more than just a search for material wealth—it is a journey of discovery, both intellectual and emotional, that challenges participants to think creatively, work together, and enjoy the adventure along the way.

Chapter 2: Common Treasure Hunt Strategies

Treasure hunting has a long history, and modern-day treasure seekers have adopted a range of strategies to maximize their chances of success. Whether searching for hidden artifacts, solving elaborate puzzles, or cracking codes, participants in treasure hunts often employ a set of proven techniques to interpret clues, recognize geographic patterns, and utilize local history and landmarks. In this chapter, we will explore these strategies and how they can be applied to Jon Collins-Black's treasure hunt, which promises hidden treasure chests worth over $2 million.

Proven Techniques for Interpreting Clues

Clue interpretation is at the heart of any treasure hunt, and successfully solving puzzles is the key to discovering hidden treasures. In modern treasure hunts like Jon Collins-Black's, clues are often layered with meaning, requiring participants to employ various techniques to decipher them. Here are some proven strategies:

1. Break Down the Language

One of the most common techniques used in treasure hunts is analyzing the language of the clues. Writers like Collins-Black often use carefully chosen words that might carry double meanings or historical references. Participants should pay close attention to every word in a clue, breaking down the sentence structure and considering alternative interpretations. For example, a clue that refers to a "rocky path" could be a literal description of a location with stones or a metaphor for a difficult journey.

In addition to word choice, treasure hunters should look for potential anagrams, wordplay, or ciphers embedded within the clue. Anagrams rearrange the letters of a word or phrase to reveal hidden meanings. This strategy requires a careful examination of the phrasing to determine whether it can be rearranged to reveal an important keyword or location.

2. Look for Symbols and Codes

In many treasure hunts, including Collins-Black's, clues are not always presented in plain text but may include symbols, visual elements, or coded messages. For example, Collins-Black's background in fantasy gaming suggests that he may incorporate cryptic symbols or even visual representations that need to be decoded.

Ciphers are another common puzzle element in treasure hunts. A cipher is a system used to encrypt and decrypt information, often requiring a key to unlock the hidden message. Common ciphers include Caesar shifts (shifting letters by a set number of positions in the alphabet) and substitution ciphers, where letters are replaced by symbols or other letters.

Treasure hunters should familiarize themselves with basic cryptographic techniques, as well as visual puzzles like rebuses (puzzles where pictures represent words or syllables). Collins-Black's clues may also contain map coordinates, time codes, or other cryptic references, so having knowledge of different codebreaking techniques can be a major advantage.

3. Study the Context of the Clues

Context is critical in interpreting treasure hunt clues. Understanding the background of the treasure, the location where it is hidden, or the narrative framework provided in a book can provide important insights. In Collins-Black's case, each clue is embedded within the broader story of *There's Treasure Inside,* meaning that understanding the book's plot, themes, and characters can be helpful when trying to decode individual clues.

Treasure hunters should also consider the time period or historical context in which the clues are set. Collins-Black has referenced historical figures such as George Washington and Jacqueline Kennedy Onassis, suggesting that his treasure chests might be located in areas with historical significance. Participants who pay attention to the historical or cultural references within the clues may be able to connect the dots more quickly.

4. Work Collaboratively

Modern treasure hunts often encourage collaboration, and Collins-Black's treasure hunt is no exception. Online communities such as Discord and Reddit have sprung up around the treasure hunt, with participants sharing their interpretations of the clues and working together to solve puzzles. In some cases, multiple perspectives can help reveal layers of meaning that might be missed when working alone.

In online forums, participants exchange theories about geographic locations, potential anagrams, or possible codes embedded within the clues. By pooling knowledge and resources, treasure hunters increase their chances of solving difficult puzzles, as multiple individuals may spot details that others overlook.

5. Think Laterally

Lateral thinking, or approaching problems from unconventional angles, is an essential skill in treasure hunting. Puzzles often require out-of-the-box thinking, where participants must set aside linear logic and look for connections between seemingly unrelated clues. Lateral thinking involves making creative leaps, such as considering that a reference to a "key" might not refer to an actual key but to something metaphorical, like an important piece of information.

In Collins-Black's treasure hunt, lateral thinking could mean connecting themes from different parts of his book to solve a puzzle or interpreting a phrase in an unexpected way. Treasure hunters who embrace lateral thinking often find hidden meanings that lead them closer to the treasure.

Geographic Patterns in Modern Treasure Hunts

In modern treasure hunts, geography often plays a critical role in solving clues and locating the hidden treasures. Understanding geographic patterns and the physical terrain of potential treasure sites can give participants a significant advantage.

1. Regional Distribution of Treasures

One of the first geographic considerations is the distribution of the treasure chests. In Collins-Black's hunt, the chests are spread across the United States, which means participants need to focus on regional clues that might help narrow down the search area. Collins-Black intentionally placed the chests in diverse locations, ensuring that treasure hunters from various parts of the country have a chance to participate.

Regional patterns often emerge through clues that reference local landmarks, natural features, or historical events. For instance, if a clue refers to the "birthplace of liberty," treasure hunters might think of Philadelphia, Pennsylvania. Similarly, references to specific types of flora and fauna can provide hints about the geographic region. A mention of redwoods, for example, might lead hunters to consider Northern California.

2. Understanding Local Geography

Once treasure hunters have a general idea of the region where a treasure might be located, they need to study the local geography in detail. This includes not only natural features like mountains, rivers, and forests but also man-made structures such as historical monuments, bridges, and roads.

In Collins-Black's treasure hunt, clues may reference topographical features or specific landmarks that are key to locating a chest. Treasure hunters should familiarize themselves with the geography of the area they are investigating, looking for any features that might align with the clues. For example, if a clue mentions a "hidden valley" or "narrow pass," participants might need to study local maps to find the location that best fits the description.

3. Geographic Patterns in Clue Design

Some treasure hunts use geographic patterns as part of the puzzle design. For example, a series of clues might lead participants on a path that traces a particular shape or symbol when mapped out. In some cases, treasure hunters have found that solving clues in sequence reveals a pattern, such as a triangle or circle, that points to the treasure's location.

Collins-Black's hunt may also involve geographic patterns hidden within the clues. For example, treasure hunters might need to visit several locations in a specific order to unlock the final clue. Studying maps and searching for patterns in the layout of potential treasure sites can be a useful strategy when trying to solve geographically-based puzzles.

The Importance of Local History and Landmarks

Local history and landmarks often play a significant role in treasure hunts, as many clues are tied to historical events, cultural references, or notable locations. In Collins-Black's treasure hunt, knowledge of local history may be crucial in solving the puzzles.

1. Historical References in Clues

Collins-Black's treasure hunt is filled with historical references, including items related to figures like George Washington and Jacqueline Kennedy Onassis. These references are not just decorative—they are often key to solving the clues and locating the treasure. Understanding the historical significance of certain places can help treasure hunters interpret the meaning behind the clues.

For example, a clue that references George Washington might point treasure hunters to Mount Vernon, his historic estate in Virginia. Similarly, a clue mentioning the Wright brothers might lead participants to Dayton, Ohio, the birthplace of aviation. By understanding the historical connections behind the clues, treasure hunters can narrow down their search to specific regions or locations.

2. The Role of Local Landmarks

Local landmarks, such as statues, monuments, or natural features, are often central to treasure hunts. In Collins-Black's hunt, participants might need to visit these landmarks to solve a puzzle or uncover a hidden clue. Landmarks often serve as waypoints, guiding treasure hunters from one location to the next until they reach the final destination.

In many cases, treasure hunters must interpret subtle clues that reference specific landmarks. For example, a clue that mentions a "towering sentinel" might refer to a tall statue or building, while a reference to a "crossroads" could point to a well-known intersection or meeting place. By visiting these landmarks and studying their significance, treasure hunters can gain valuable insights into the puzzle.

3. Using Historical Maps and Documents

Historical maps and documents are invaluable resources for treasure hunters. Old maps often contain information about landmarks, buildings, or natural features that no longer exist in the modern landscape but are referenced in the clues. Collins-Black's treasure hunt may include such references, requiring participants to dig into historical archives to find old maps or documents that provide clues to the treasure's location.

Additionally, treasure hunters should pay attention to the historical context of the region they are exploring. In some cases, clues may reference events from a particular time period, requiring knowledge of local history to understand their significance. For example, a clue that mentions the "Great Fire" might refer to a famous fire in a specific city, guiding treasure hunters to the location of a historical marker commemorating the event.

In Jon Collins-Black's treasure hunt, success depends on a combination of careful clue interpretation, geographic knowledge, and understanding of local history. By employing proven strategies like

breaking down language, studying symbols and codes, recognizing geographic patterns, and utilizing historical landmarks, treasure hunters can increase their chances of discovering one of the hidden chests. The adventure is not only about solving puzzles but also about learning more about the world around us—geographically, historically, and culturally.

Chapter 3: Decoding Clues: A Strategic Approach

In modern treasure hunts like Jon Collins-Black's multi-million dollar chest challenge, the clues are often complex, layered, and require deep analysis to decipher. Fortunately, treasure hunters don't need to buy the book *There's Treasure Inside* to start decoding the hints and making progress toward finding the hidden chests. In this chapter, we will explore strategic methods for decoding clues by leveraging free resources, crowdsourcing information from online communities, and reverse-engineering known locations to unlock further hints. This approach allows for a thoughtful, systematic effort without needing to purchase the guide itself, all while staying within ethical boundaries.

How to Approach the Book Without Buying It

The first question many treasure hunters face is how to gather vital information from Jon Collins-Black's treasure hunt without purchasing the book. While it's essential not to violate any copyright laws or ethics, there are several ways to approach the hunt based on secondary resources, including media articles, interviews, summaries, and other participants' discussions.

1. Leverage Publicly Available Summaries and Reviews

One effective way to get an overview of the treasure hunt without buying the book is by relying on publicly available summaries and reviews. Many media outlets, such as CNN, have covered Collins-Black's treasure hunt, providing insights into his motivations, the scope of the project, and even some broad clues and themes. Review websites, online articles, and blog posts often summarize key points from the book, allowing treasure hunters to pick up essential details without purchasing it.

Collins-Black's treasure hunt has garnered significant public attention, and several treasure-hunting blogs and communities regularly discuss the book's content. These sources can offer important excerpts, high-level summaries of each chapter, or reflections on how the clues work, giving participants a head start. Keeping an eye on reputable news outlets and blogs that focus on treasure hunting will allow you to glean critical information.

2. Analyze Interviews with Collins-Black

Jon Collins-Black has given interviews in which he talks about the treasure hunt's inspiration, his thought process behind the clues, and some thematic elements of the book. By studying these interviews, treasure hunters can learn valuable information about how he designed the puzzles and what types of locations he considered when hiding the chests. Often, treasure hunters can pick up on subtle hints the author may drop during interviews that could give an advantage in solving the puzzles.

For example, interviews with Collins-Black may reveal his admiration for particular regions or historical events, offering insight into potential treasure locations. By closely analyzing his language, enthusiasm, or offhand comments, treasure hunters can begin to build hypotheses about where the chests might be hidden.

3. Use Secondary Sources for Clue Context

In treasure hunts, many of the clues are contextual, relying on the broader story or themes provided in the book. Luckily, this context can often be found in secondary sources, including articles, summaries, and discussions about the treasure hunt. Understanding the main themes—such as the importance of history, puzzles, or certain cultural references—allows hunters to approximate what types of clues Collins-Black may include and where the treasures might be hidden.

By researching common themes in his previous work and the inspirations he has mentioned, treasure hunters can start to understand the kind of narratives or puzzles that might arise in the hunt, even without the full text of the book in hand.

Crowdsourcing Information: Using Online Communities and Forums

In the age of digital collaboration, treasure hunting has evolved from a solitary pursuit to a collective effort. Online communities and forums, including platforms like Reddit and Discord, have become central hubs for treasure hunters to share their findings, theories, and interpretations of the clues. These digital communities are essential for gathering information, discussing strategies, and brainstorming potential solutions in a collaborative environment.

1. Participating in Treasure-Hunting Forums

Treasure hunting forums, such as the ones on Reddit, often have dedicated threads where participants exchange information and theories about ongoing hunts, including Collins-Black's. These forums are treasure troves of knowledge, offering insights into clues, geographical details, and puzzle-solving strategies. While some participants may have already purchased the book, they often share what they've learned, including summaries of key chapters or clues.

By participating actively in these discussions, treasure hunters can build on the work of others, helping to fill in the gaps and offering interpretations that others might not have considered. Forums also tend to attract participants from various backgrounds, including history buffs, geographers, and puzzle enthusiasts, which means there is a wealth of specialized knowledge to tap into.

2. Joining Discord Servers for Real-Time Collaboration

Discord servers dedicated to treasure hunts provide real-time discussion and collaboration. These servers often have hundreds, if not thousands, of members actively engaged in deciphering clues, exchanging ideas, and analyzing possible treasure locations. Because of the fast-paced nature of Discord chats, participants can quickly share new discoveries, theories, and even images of potential clue sites.

In some treasure hunts, Discord members have organized local search teams to physically investigate suspected locations, adding a crucial on-the-ground element to the collaborative effort. By staying connected to these groups, treasure hunters can follow up on leads they may not be able to pursue themselves due to geographic distance or time constraints.

3. Cross-Referencing Clue Interpretations

One of the most valuable aspects of online communities is the ability to cross-reference different interpretations of the same clues. Collins-Black's clues are designed to be complex and multi-layered, so participants will often approach them from various angles. By comparing different interpretations, treasure hunters can identify common threads or recurring themes that might be the key to unlocking a clue.

For example, if multiple forum participants independently arrive at the same conclusion about a certain geographic feature or historical reference, it could signal a breakthrough in solving that particular puzzle. Likewise, contrasting interpretations can highlight alternative possibilities or areas that others may have overlooked.

Reverse-Engineering Hints Based on Known Treasure Locations

One of the most advanced strategies in modern treasure hunting is reverse-engineering. This approach involves examining known treasure locations, analyzing the clues that led to their discovery, and using that information to extrapolate how other clues might function. Since Collins-Black's treasure chests are hidden in diverse locations across the United States, treasure hunters can begin by studying the clues that have already been solved and applying similar logic to other unsolved puzzles.

1. Analyzing Solved Clues for Patterns

When a treasure chest is discovered, it provides invaluable insight into how Collins-Black structures his clues. By analyzing the sequence of clues that led to a specific chest, treasure hunters can begin to identify patterns in the wording, geography, and historical references that are common across the puzzles. This can reveal recurring motifs or thematic elements that might appear in other treasure locations.

For example, if a clue in a previously discovered treasure referred to a specific historical event or landmark, treasure hunters can infer that Collins-Black may be using similar historical references for other hidden chests. By cataloging these references and patterns, hunters can create a framework for interpreting new clues.

2. Reverse-Engineering from Geography

Geography often plays a central role in treasure hunts, as clues frequently reference natural landmarks, regional features, or local history. Once a treasure location has been identified, treasure hunters should closely examine the geographical elements that led to its discovery. What kind of landmarks were involved? Was there a particular type of terrain or environmental feature that played a role in solving the puzzle?

By understanding the geographic characteristics of known treasure locations, hunters can reverse-engineer the logic Collins-Black uses to hide his treasures. This could involve analyzing maps, studying local terrain, or considering the proximity of major landmarks to suspected treasure locations.

3. Applying Historical References to New Clue

Many treasure hunts, including Collins-Black's, rely heavily on historical references to guide treasure hunters toward specific locations. Once a treasure has been found, hunters should pay close attention to the historical figures, events, or objects associated with that particular location. Reverse-engineering this historical reference can provide a model for solving new clues, especially if similar historical themes appear in multiple puzzles.

For instance, if one treasure chest was found near a historically significant site connected to the American Revolution, treasure hunters might begin to consider other important locations from that era as potential sites for additional chests. This process of cross-referencing historical contexts with known treasure locations allows hunters to narrow their focus and create targeted strategies for solving unsolved clues.

Decoding the clues in Jon Collins-Black's treasure hunt requires a blend of strategic thinking, collaboration, and careful analysis. By approaching the hunt without purchasing the book, treasure hunters can leverage publicly available information, tap into the collective intelligence of online communities, and use reverse-engineering techniques to solve puzzles based on known treasure locations. The key to success lies in methodically applying these strategies, remaining adaptable, and utilizing every available resource to uncover the hidden treasures waiting to be discovered.

Chapter 4: The Power of Collaboration

In the realm of modern treasure hunts, collaboration has become an essential tool for uncovering hidden riches. Whether it's Jon Collins-Black's multi-million-dollar treasure chests or other high-stakes hunts, working together is often the key to decoding complex clues and finding success. The internet has transformed treasure hunting from an individual quest into a collective effort, enabling people from all over the world to share ideas, cross-reference theories, and collectively analyze data. In this chapter, we will explore the tools and platforms that facilitate group problem-solving and collaboration, as well as the benefits of working together in treasure hunts.

Tools for Group Problem Solving

Group problem-solving is a process that involves multiple people contributing their skills, knowledge, and perspectives to achieve a common goal. When it comes to treasure hunts, group collaboration allows for the pooling of resources—such as geographic knowledge, puzzle-solving expertise, and access to local historical data—that no single person could possess alone. Here are some tools that help groups solve problems more efficiently in treasure hunts:

1. Digital Mapping Software

One of the most important tools for treasure hunters working in groups is digital mapping software. Programs like Google Maps, Google Earth, and ArcGIS provide the capability to map out potential treasure locations, study geographic clues, and chart progress as theories are tested. Treasure hunters can overlay historical maps, geographical features, and land use data to better understand clues that might be related to specific locations.

For instance, many treasure hunts involve geographic clues tied to specific regions or landmarks. By using digital mapping tools, treasure hunters can visualize the landscape from multiple perspectives—historical, topographical, and even satellite views.

Teams working together on digital maps can place pins on suspected locations, mark off areas that have already been searched, and highlight patterns in the clues.

2. Collaborative Whiteboards

Collaborative whiteboards, such as Miro or Jamboard, allow treasure hunters to brainstorm ideas in real-time, regardless of their geographic location. These platforms provide a digital space where users can write, draw, and post images, facilitating the kind of creative thinking that is often necessary for solving complex puzzles. Teams can sketch out maps, write down potential clues, and even share photos of sites they've visited, making it easier for everyone to contribute.

One of the advantages of collaborative whiteboards is that they are highly visual, allowing hunters to see the big picture. This visualization helps teams connect seemingly unrelated clues or recognize patterns they might have missed when working in isolation. By keeping all ideas in one space, whiteboards also ensure that no piece of information gets lost or forgotten during the collaborative process.

3. Shared Document Platforms

For treasure hunters who prefer a more structured approach to collaboration, shared document platforms like Google Docs or Microsoft OneDrive provide an effective solution. These platforms allow multiple users to work on the same document simultaneously, enabling teams to compile theories, organize clues, and track progress in an organized manner.

Shared documents can serve as centralized hubs for information, where hunters document each clue, theory, and potential solution. Since these platforms allow for version control and commenting, team members can leave notes for each other, suggest improvements, and ensure that all contributions are preserved. This method is particularly useful for treasure hunts that require long-term commitment and extensive analysis.

4. Messaging and Communication Tools

Effective communication is the backbone of any successful collaboration, and messaging tools like Slack, Microsoft Teams, and Discord are essential for keeping the team connected. These tools allow groups to create dedicated channels for specific topics, such as particular clues, geographic regions, or solved puzzles. With real-time messaging, team members can discuss theories, share updates, and ask for feedback on their ideas.

Additionally, these platforms often include features for voice or video calls, which can be invaluable for more complex discussions or when the team needs to brainstorm together. The ability to share files, images, and links directly in the chat stream makes it easier to cross-reference information and ensure that everyone has access to the same resources.

Platforms for Discussion (Discord, Reddit, etc.)

In the digital age, dedicated online platforms for discussion have become powerful tools for treasure hunters seeking to collaborate on large-scale hunts like Jon Collins-Black's. These platforms provide spaces where hunters from around the world can exchange theories, compare research, and form teams to tackle specific aspects of the treasure hunt. Two of the most popular platforms for this type of collaboration are Discord and Reddit.

1. Discord: Real-Time Collaboration

Discord has emerged as one of the most popular platforms for real-time collaboration in treasure hunting communities. Originally designed for gamers, Discord offers a wide range of features that make it an ideal space for treasure hunters to gather, communicate, and share ideas. The platform allows users to create dedicated servers—each with its own set of channels—where discussions can be organized by topic, region, or clue.

For example, a Discord server dedicated to Jon Collins-Black's treasure hunt might include separate channels for discussing each of the five treasure chests, as well as general chat rooms for brainstorming, sharing updates, and even organizing meetups for local searches. Discord's real-time nature means that users can engage in live conversations, ask questions, and immediately get feedback from other participants.

Discord also supports voice and video chat, which can be useful for more detailed discussions or when teams need to review maps, photos, or other visual clues together. This flexibility makes Discord one of the most effective platforms for collaborative problem-solving in real-time.

2. Reddit: Asynchronous Discussion and Idea Sharing

While Discord is ideal for real-time interaction, Reddit excels at asynchronous discussion. Reddit's structure—based on posts and comment threads—allows users to present detailed theories, ask for feedback, and respond to others' ideas at their own pace. The platform's upvoting system ensures that the most useful and popular contributions rise to the top, helping users quickly identify the most promising theories and strategies.

Subreddits (dedicated forums within Reddit) focused on treasure hunts provide a space for long-form discussion and analysis. In the case of Collins-Black's treasure hunt, a dedicated subreddit might host threads discussing each treasure chest, along with additional posts that dissect specific clues, geographic features, or puzzle-solving techniques. Users can post photos of potential treasure locations, share historical research, and debate the meaning of specific clues.

One of Reddit's strengths is its community-driven nature. Many users contribute to crowdsourced databases of information, such as Google Sheets or maps, that everyone can access and contribute to. This collective effort ensures that no clue is overlooked and that information is constantly being refined and updated.

3. Facebook Groups and Other Social Media Platforms

In addition to Discord and Reddit, Facebook Groups remain popular platforms for treasure-hunting communities. These groups tend to attract a more diverse audience, often including individuals who might not be as familiar with Reddit or Discord. Facebook Groups allow users to post updates, share photos, and comment on others' posts, but they also have more of a social media feel, with participants often sharing personal stories or experiences related to their treasure-hunting adventures.

While Facebook Groups don't offer the same level of organization or real-time collaboration as Discord, they provide a more casual and accessible space for people to join the conversation. Many treasure hunters participate in multiple platforms—using Discord for real-time discussions, Reddit for in-depth analysis, and Facebook Groups for general updates and social interactions.

Analyzing the Best Theories and Collaborating on Maps

One of the most significant benefits of collaboration in treasure hunting is the ability to analyze and refine theories collectively. By working together, treasure hunters can cross-reference each other's ideas, test different hypotheses, and ultimately arrive at more informed conclusions. Mapping is often central to this process, as clues are frequently tied to specific geographic locations.

1. The Importance of Theories in Treasure Hunting

In complex treasure hunts like Collins-Black's, theories are often built on layers of information, from geographic clues to historical references to wordplay. A single treasure chest might have dozens of competing theories surrounding its location, with each one based on a different interpretation of the clues. Collaborative teams work together to refine these theories, debating their merits and testing their validity.

For example, if a clue references a historical figure or event, team members might conduct research to verify the connection and determine how it could point to a specific location. Others might focus on interpreting wordplay or decoding cryptic symbols in the clues. By pooling their skills, teams can narrow down the possibilities and eliminate less likely theories.

2. Collaborating on Maps

Mapping plays a crucial role in treasure hunting, especially when clues reference specific landmarks, geographic features, or historical locations. Collaborative map tools, such as Google Maps or custom mapping platforms like ZeeMaps, allow treasure hunters to mark potential treasure locations, annotate clues, and track progress as they test different theories.

Teams working together on a map can layer different types of information—such as topography, historical sites, and transportation routes—onto a single map, creating a comprehensive view of the region. This approach helps hunters visualize how clues might fit together geographically and identify patterns that might not be apparent from clues alone.

By cross-referencing maps with other data sources—such as historical records, local legends, or geographic surveys—teams can create a detailed picture of potential treasure sites, making it easier to focus their search efforts.

3. Testing and Refining Theories

Once a team has developed a theory and mapped out potential treasure locations, the next step is to test and refine it. This might involve sending a local team member to investigate a site in person, or using digital tools to conduct further research and analysis. Teams frequently iterate on their theories, refining them based on new information or feedback from other participants.

The collective process of testing and refining theories ensures that no detail is overlooked and that the most promising clues are pursued first. As theories evolve, teams often share their findings with the broader community, helping others refine their own searches.

Collaboration is one of the most powerful tools available to modern treasure hunters, enabling them to pool their resources, share knowledge, and collectively solve the complex puzzles that lead to hidden riches. With the right tools—ranging from digital maps to collaborative whiteboards to online discussion platforms like Discord and

Reddit—teams can work together to decode clues, cross-reference theories, and map out potential treasure locations. By leveraging the power of collaboration, treasure hunters increase their chances of success, unlocking new insights and ultimately bringing them closer to their goal.

Chapter 5: Historical and Cultural Connections

In the realm of treasure hunts like Jon Collins-Black's, historical and cultural connections are often at the heart of the puzzles. These connections can reveal not only the inspiration behind the treasure but also provide clues that lead directly to the locations of the chests. Understanding the historical significance of the artifacts in the chests and the figures and events referenced in the clues can make the difference between stumbling blindly through the hunt and solving the mysteries with precision.

This chapter will explore the historical and cultural aspects embedded in Collins-Black's treasure hunt, and how they serve as both thematic elements and practical hints to guide participants toward success. We'll delve into the significance of artifacts hidden in the chests, examine key historical figures likely referenced in the clues, and show how conducting targeted historical research can be one of the most effective strategies for locating a treasure.

The Significance of Artifacts in the Chests

One of the most captivating elements of treasure hunts like Collins-Black's is the promise of not just wealth, but also the discovery of rare and culturally significant artifacts. In many modern treasure hunts, including this one, the contents of the chests are designed to carry deep historical significance, representing either specific moments in time or important cultural milestones.

Artifacts as Storytellers

Artifacts within treasure chests often tell a story, offering insight into the themes and inspirations of the hunt. For example, the items hidden in Jon Collins-Black's chests might include ancient coins, maps, letters, or relics that serve as a tangible connection to historical periods or legendary events. These objects are not random collectibles—they are carefully chosen to align with the clues leading to the treasure.

By examining the possible significance of these artifacts, hunters can reverse-engineer the logic behind the hunt. A chest that contains an 18th-century map, for example, might point hunters toward a location with historical relevance to that time period, such as a colonial settlement or a famous voyage. Likewise, a rare coin minted in a specific country might provide clues about geographic connections or economic history.

Symbolic and Cultural Importance

The artifacts in Collins-Black's chests may also carry symbolic meaning, reflecting broader cultural narratives. In treasure hunts, symbolic artifacts—such as specific gemstones, religious symbols, or weapons—often link to legends, myths, or historical movements. These items are sometimes chosen for their ability to evoke a particular culture or era, encouraging treasure hunters to investigate the cultural heritage of the regions or peoples referenced in the clues.

For example, if a chest contains a Viking-era sword, it might point to locations that have historical significance in Norse culture. Similarly, if a chest includes Native American pottery or tools, the treasure might be hidden on or near land that holds historical and cultural importance to indigenous peoples.

Understanding these cultural and symbolic connections can provide treasure hunters with key insights into both the location of the treasure and the broader narrative behind the hunt. In this way, the artifacts in the chests not only serve as rewards for finding the treasure but also as clues in their own right.

Key Historical Figures to Watch Out For

Historical figures often play an important role in treasure hunts, either as direct subjects of the clues or as thematic inspirations behind the hunt. In Jon Collins-Black's treasure hunt, it is likely that key historical figures—famous explorers, political leaders, or cultural icons—will be referenced in the clues, either overtly or subtly.

Historical Figures as Clue Subjects

In many treasure hunts, clues reference specific historical figures whose actions, discoveries, or legacies provide hints about the location of the treasure. These figures might be famous explorers, adventurers, or even local historical figures whose significance has been preserved through local legends or archival documents.

For example, if one of Collins-Black's clues references someone like Christopher Columbus or Sir Francis Drake, it could point to a location connected with their voyages or discoveries. Similarly, clues might reference lesser-known historical figures who played key roles in regional history, such as indigenous leaders or early settlers. These figures could provide geographic or cultural clues about the regions where the treasure is hidden.

Mythological or Legendary Figures

In addition to historical figures, many treasure hunts also draw inspiration from mythological or legendary characters. These figures, while not necessarily rooted in documented history, carry cultural significance that can guide hunters toward important locations or themes. Mythical heroes, gods, or folklore icons are often associated with specific regions or natural features, and understanding the cultural stories behind these figures can unlock vital clues.

For example, if one of Collins-Black's clues references figures from Greek mythology, like Perseus or Heracles, hunters might investigate locations tied to ancient Greek history or legendary journeys. Similarly, references to figures from Native American or Celtic mythology could direct treasure hunters toward culturally important landmarks or geographic features like rivers, mountains, or ceremonial sites.

By recognizing these historical or mythological figures in the clues, hunters can narrow down the list of potential treasure locations based on the geographical or cultural significance of the individuals or characters referenced.

How Historical Research Can Lead You to a Chest Location

One of the most effective strategies for locating treasure in a hunt like Collins-Black's is to conduct targeted historical research. Treasure hunts that involve intricate puzzles and clues often require a deep understanding of history, geography, and cultural heritage in order to solve them.

Hunters who take the time to research key historical events, figures, and locations will gain a significant advantage in interpreting the clues and mapping out potential treasure sites.

1. Understanding the Time Periods Referenced in the Clues

Many treasure hunts, including Collins-Black's, rely heavily on references to specific historical periods, which provide context for the clues. These time periods often reflect significant events in regional history, such as wars, economic booms, or exploratory expeditions. Clues might reference these events either directly or indirectly, requiring hunters to dig into the history of the region to fully understand their significance.

For example, if a clue references a "golden age" or a "revolutionary year," it could point to periods of prosperity or conflict in the region, such as the Gold Rush or the American Revolution. By researching the events that took place during these time periods, treasure hunters can narrow down potential locations based on their historical importance.

Additionally, references to less obvious historical periods—such as the Renaissance, the Industrial Revolution, or the Cold War—can provide important context for the clues. By understanding how these periods influenced the development of certain regions or cities, hunters can better interpret the clues and focus their search on areas that hold historical significance from those times.

2. Identifying Important Historical Landmarks

Historical landmarks often play a central role in treasure hunts, serving as geographic anchors for the clues. Many of these landmarks have cultural or political significance, making them ideal locations for hiding treasure or for providing critical clues about the treasure's location. Landmarks can range from ancient ruins to colonial forts, from famous battlefields to iconic buildings or bridges.

In Collins-Black's treasure hunt, clues might reference well-known landmarks—such as the Liberty Bell, the Statue of Liberty, or

Mount Rushmore—or they might point to lesser-known historical sites that hold local significance. These locations could be related to specific historical events, such as battles, treaties, or migrations, and understanding the importance of these events can help treasure hunters pinpoint likely treasure locations.

3. Utilizing Archival Documents and Historical Maps

Another powerful tool for treasure hunters is the use of archival documents and historical maps. Many treasure hunts include clues that are either based on or directly reference old maps, deeds, or letters. These documents often contain subtle geographic or linguistic clues that can guide hunters toward the treasure, but they require careful analysis to interpret correctly.

For example, an old map might include place names that no longer exist or reference geographic features that have since changed due to natural or human alterations. By cross-referencing these old maps with modern tools like Google Earth or GIS software, treasure hunters can identify how the landscape has changed over time and locate hidden sites that match the descriptions in the clues.

In some cases, clues might reference archival documents such as letters, newspapers, or government records that contain coded information about the treasure's location. For instance, a letter written by a historical figure might include veiled references to a hidden location, requiring hunters to conduct detailed research into the writer's life, travels, or associations in order to fully understand the clue.

4. Cross-Referencing Clues with Local History

Finally, one of the most valuable research strategies is to cross-reference the clues with local history. Many treasure hunts are deeply rooted in the culture and history of specific regions, and clues often reference local legends, folklore, or famous events. By researching the local history of the areas where the treasure is suspected to be hidden, hunters can gain valuable insights into the cultural and geographic context of the clues.

For example, if a clue references a "legendary king" or a "forgotten hero," hunters might investigate local legends or historical figures whose stories are still told in the area. Likewise, clues that reference specific natural features—such as rivers, mountains, or forests—might be tied to local stories or events, providing hints about where to search.

Local historical societies, museums, and archives are excellent resources for treasure hunters conducting this type of research. Many of these institutions have extensive collections of regional history, including maps, letters, and oral histories that can provide crucial insights into the clues.

The historical and cultural connections embedded in treasure hunts like Jon Collins-Black's are essential for unlocking the puzzles and locating the treasure. By understanding the significance of the artifacts in the chests, recognizing key historical and mythological figures in the clues, and conducting targeted historical research, treasure hunters can gain a deeper understanding of the hunt and increase their chances of success. Whether through studying historical maps, analyzing archival documents, or investigating local legends, treasure hunters who take the time to delve into the past will be rewarded with the knowledge they need to solve the mysteries and discover the hidden treasure.

Chapter 6: Geographic Locations and Possible Hints

In treasure hunts like Jon Collins-Black's, geographic locations play a pivotal role in guiding participants toward the chests. The treasure hunt's clues often relate directly to terrain features, national landmarks, and historical sites, which all form essential parts of the puzzle. Understanding these elements—and how they are embedded in the clues—is key to unlocking the location of the treasure. This chapter explores how geographic locations, terrain-based clues, and patterns in treasure placement across the U.S. can lead to the discovery of hidden chests.

We will begin by examining how terrain and geography play into the treasure hunt and why national parks and historical sites are likely targets for hiding treasure. From there, we'll explore patterns in treasure placement and how geographic research can be one of the most effective strategies for pinpointing where these chests might lie.

Understanding Terrain-Based Clues

One of the most intriguing aspects of treasure hunts is how they often rely on subtle geographic cues, particularly in terrain-based clues. These clues may reference natural landscapes, topographic features, or specific environmental characteristics that help narrow down the treasure's location.

Topographic Features and Landmarks

Topography plays a central role in treasure hunts because natural features are often among the most enduring landmarks that stand the test of time. In Jon Collins-Black's treasure hunt, clues are likely to involve the identification of specific terrain elements like mountains, rivers, lakes, valleys, and forests. For example, a clue might reference a "ridge that catches the first light of dawn" or "a river that winds like a serpent." These clues are rooted in geographic features and require a deep understanding of the landscape.

Topographic features such as hills, valleys, and ridges can help hunters understand not only the physical location of a chest but also the environment surrounding it. For instance, if a clue refers to a specific elevation or a body of water that is "hidden from view by towering peaks," treasure hunters might look for a region where such a topographic feature exists—whether it be a remote mountain pass or a secluded valley.

Geographic Coordinates and Directions

Another common tactic in treasure hunts is to use directional language in the clues, such as "toward the rising sun" (east) or "where the sun sets behind the mountains" (west). While these directional clues can often be interpreted in multiple ways, they provide a starting point for determining geographic location. Combining these directions with specific geographic features allows hunters to trace a path, much like using a compass or a map.

In some cases, clues may directly reference longitude and latitude coordinates, providing the most explicit guidance toward a specific location. Even if explicit coordinates are not provided, hunters should be aware that many treasure hunts incorporate maps, geocaching tools, or geographic software that may allow them to pinpoint exact locations when combined with other clues.

National Parks and Historical Sites: Likely Targets?

National parks and historical sites are often chosen as locations for treasure hunts due to their historical significance, accessibility, and the variety of terrain they cover. These places are typically known for their natural beauty and cultural importance, making them prime candidates for hiding treasure. Collins-Black's hunt, which spans across the United States, is likely to involve clues that lead participants to such significant sites, from coastal landmarks to mountain ranges and historic towns.

National Parks as Prime Locations

National parks across the U.S. are rich in both natural beauty and cultural history, making them ideal locations for treasure hunts. Parks like Yellowstone, Yosemite, the Grand Canyon, and the Great Smoky Mountains offer varied landscapes—ranging from vast canyons and towering cliffs to serene lakes and deep forests—that make them suitable for embedding hidden treasures. These locations are often chosen for treasure hunts because they are not only stunning and iconic but also contain many secluded or less-explored areas that could hide treasure chests out of sight from the general public.

For example, a clue referencing “a river that runs through the heart of a canyon” could point hunters toward the Colorado River in the Grand Canyon, or “a waterfall with mist that kisses the earth” might lead to one of the many waterfalls in Yosemite. Knowing the geographic features of national parks can provide vital insight into where a chest may be hidden. It is also likely that these parks have ties to historical events, such as the Native American heritage in the Grand

Canyon or the Civil War history of Gettysburg National Park, which could further inform hunters of potential treasure locations.

Historical Sites and Landmarks

In addition to national parks, historical sites—whether they are battlefields, former colonial settlements, or notable landmarks—also play an important role in the hunt. These sites hold significant historical value, often marking critical moments in the formation of the United States, and treasure hunters will find that many of Collins-Black's clues are likely to reference such places.

For example, a clue may mention the "first place where a nation was born" or a "battle fought under the flag of liberty." This could direct participants toward places like Independence Hall in Philadelphia or the Boston Tea Party Ships and Museum, both of which are deeply intertwined with the birth of the nation. Other sites of historical significance, like Civil War battlefields or pioneer settlements, may be referenced through clues that evoke pivotal moments in American history.

The value of historical sites in treasure hunts lies not just in their geographic or cultural significance but in the extensive documentation and records about these places, which can offer hunters valuable contextual information. Historical maps, diaries, and records are often linked to these sites, and exploring the history behind these landmarks can yield vital clues.

Patterns in the Treasure's Placement Across the U.S.

Understanding the geographic patterns in the placement of Collins-Black's treasure chests is crucial to narrowing down search areas. While the treasure could theoretically be hidden anywhere, there are several possible patterns that can be observed in the placement of such chests.

Regional Distribution and Accessibility

Collins-Black's decision to hide five chests across the United States means that the locations are likely to be spread out geographically, covering different regions of the country. By studying the general geography of the U.S., participants can make educated guesses about where the treasure might be located based on regional diversity, terrain, and cultural landmarks.

For example, one chest may be located in the rugged terrains of the Rocky Mountains, while another could be hidden in the wooded forests of the Pacific Northwest. A third treasure may be located in the historical towns of the Northeast, and another may be hidden along the shores of the Great Lakes or the Gulf Coast. Given Collins-Black's emphasis on making the hunt accessible, it's likely that the treasure locations are chosen to reflect a balance of natural beauty and accessibility, ensuring that participants from across the country can take part in the hunt.

Clues Based on Natural Formations and Patterns

Another potential pattern to observe is the relationship between geographic clues and natural formations. In many treasure hunts, the clues will reference the geography in ways that may highlight natural formations like mountain ranges, river systems, or geological features. For instance, if a chest is hidden near the Mississippi River, clues may mention the "mighty flow of water" or "where the river divides the land." Similarly, a chest hidden in the Rocky Mountains may reference "where the peaks kiss the sky" or "in the shadow of the highest summit."

These geographic features not only provide directional clues but also hint at the relative positioning of the chests across the country. The placement of the chests is likely to follow an underlying geographic logic—whether that's moving from east to west or aligning with a series of historical events that occurred at certain locations.

Clues that Connect Locations

Finally, many treasure hunts include clues that connect specific locations, creating a network of sites that must be explored in a particular order. Collins-Black's treasure hunt could employ this technique, with clues linking one chest's location to another, perhaps along famous trails, highways, or routes. Participants may need to travel between these sites to decode the hunt's final message. For instance, the first clue could lead to a site in the Northeast, with subsequent clues pointing toward a location in the Midwest, and so on, until the final chest is found.

This method not only adds an element of adventure and exploration but also creates a sense of narrative continuity as participants follow a series of clues that reveal more about America's geography and history with each stop along the way.

Geographic locations and terrain-based clues are essential elements in the treasure hunt experience, especially in hunts like Collins-Black's. Understanding the landscape, terrain features, and historic landmarks can significantly narrow down search areas, giving participants the tools to decode the clues more effectively. National parks, historical sites, and natural landmarks are prime targets for hidden treasures, as they offer the perfect combination of accessibility, historical significance, and natural beauty. By recognizing geographic patterns, researching significant locations, and paying attention to terrain-based clues, treasure hunters can gain a competitive edge in the race to uncover the hidden chests. The search is not just about discovering treasure—it's about exploring the rich geography and history of the United States, piece by piece, until the treasure is found.

Chapter 7: Avoiding Red Herrings

In any treasure hunt, one of the most challenging and frustrating obstacles is dealing with red herrings—false leads that can derail your progress and cause you to waste valuable time and effort. As you embark on a journey to discover hidden treasure, understanding how to identify and avoid these misleading clues is crucial to staying on track. In this chapter, we will explore how to recognize red herrings, how to stay focused on genuine clues, and the balance between overthinking and underthinking, which can cloud your judgment and prevent you from successfully solving the puzzle.

Identifying False Leads

False leads, or red herrings, are deliberately misleading clues that may seem important but ultimately lead you down the wrong path. In a well-designed treasure hunt like the one created by Jon Collins-Black, red herrings are often strategically placed to challenge hunters' problem-solving skills and force them to think critically. While they can be frustrating, red herrings are an integral part of the puzzle-solving process, as they encourage you to question your assumptions and refine your methods.

Common Types of Red Herrings

1. **Misleading Language:** A common technique for creating red herrings is through the use of vague or

ambiguous language. Clues that are open to multiple interpretations can easily lead hunters astray. For example, a clue might say, “Follow the path where the sun rises in the morning,” which could lead you to assume it means east, but it could be a metaphorical clue rather than a literal direction. Being aware of such ambiguous language and questioning whether a clue is too vague to be actionable is important in separating false leads from genuine ones.

2. **Excessive Detail:** In some cases, red herrings are created by providing an overload of details, many of which may seem significant but are

ultimately unnecessary. This can occur when a clue is filled with descriptions of unimportant landmarks, objects, or events. For example, a clue may describe the exact height of a mountain or the color of a building in great detail, which may seem like critical information but does not actually help lead to the treasure. When faced with such details, you should ask yourself if the information is truly helpful or if it's designed to distract you.

3. **Contradictory Clues:** Another common red herring is the presence of contradictory clues. These clues often directly conflict with one another and

lead hunters to believe they must reconcile the differences in some way. For example, one clue might suggest that the treasure is hidden "in the shadow of the mountain," while another implies it is hidden "in the valley to the south." These contradictions are meant to confuse participants and divert them from focusing on the actual location. When you encounter contradictory clues, it's important to step back and reassess your interpretation of the puzzle.

4. **Excessive Focus on Unimportant Locations:** Red herrings often focus attention on unimportant or irrelevant locations. For example, a clue might

direct you toward a well-known city or landmark, but this location might not actually be connected to the treasure. In treasure hunts like Collins-Black's, where many chests are hidden across the United States, it's essential to recognize when a clue might be highlighting a famous but irrelevant location. This can often lead to hours of searching in places that have no connection to the treasure chest.

The Role of Red Herrings in Collins-Black's Hunt

In Jon Collins-Black's treasure hunt, red herrings serve a specific purpose: they force participants to think critically and test their assumptions. While this may seem frustrating at times, the presence of these misleading clues is part of what makes the hunt so intellectually engaging. Collins-Black has crafted a series of clues that require hunters to use logic and reasoning, encouraging them to consider multiple interpretations and eliminate the misleading ones. When red herrings are encountered, it's crucial to remain calm, take a step back, and avoid jumping to conclusions based on false leads.

How to Stay Focused on Genuine Clues

Amidst the false leads, it's important to focus on the genuine clues—those that will ultimately guide you to the hidden chest. Staying focused requires a combination of patience, persistence, and a methodical approach to problem-solving. Here are a few strategies for ensuring that you stay on track and avoid getting bogged down by red herrings.

Break Down the Clue

The first step to identifying a genuine clue is to break it down into smaller parts. Look for specific pieces of information that are actionable or concrete. For example, if a clue references a landmark or a natural feature, focus on those specific references rather than attempting to interpret broader, less definitive details. Breaking down clues into digestible pieces can help you hone in on the important elements and avoid being distracted by irrelevant information.

Consistency is Key

A genuine clue will usually be consistent with other parts of the puzzle, whether that's through repeated references to certain locations, objects, or themes. Take note of recurring elements in the clues and see if they align with each other. For example, if multiple clues point to the same general area or reference the same landmark, it's a good indication that you're on the right track. By tracking these connections, you can build a coherent understanding of the puzzle and filter out false leads.

Eliminate the Impossible

When faced with a seemingly challenging clue, it's essential to eliminate impossible solutions. If a clue leads you to an area that contradicts what you already know about the terrain, or if it suggests a location that seems physically impossible to access, it's likely a red herring. For example, if a clue suggests that a chest is hidden underwater in a location that's only accessible by an expensive private boat, it might be a false lead. By systematically eliminating impossible scenarios, you can reduce the number of potential locations to explore.

Stay Organized

Another effective way to stay focused on genuine clues is to stay organized. Maintain a detailed record of all the clues you have gathered, along with your interpretations and potential locations. This can help you track patterns, eliminate contradictions, and ensure that you're not overlooking important clues. Keeping a map or diagram of potential locations can also be helpful in visualizing where each clue leads and identifying connections between clues.

The Balance Between Overthinking and Underthinking

One of the most difficult aspects of a treasure hunt is maintaining the right balance between overthinking and underthinking clues. Both extremes can lead to mistakes that slow you down or prevent you from making progress.

Overthinking: Reading Too Much into the Clues

Overthinking occurs when you place too much significance on certain details or try to connect every piece of information in a way that might not be intended. This often leads to convoluted theories that are disconnected from the actual solution. For example, if a clue refers to the "oldest oak tree in the forest," overthinking might cause you to analyze every oak tree in a particular forest, even though the clue might not refer to a literal tree at all. In these cases, it's essential to step back and ask yourself whether the interpretation is realistic and consistent with the rest of the clues.

The key to avoiding overthinking is to stay grounded in logic. While it's tempting to dive deep into every possible connection, remember that the clues are likely designed to lead you in a specific direction. Keep your interpretations simple and focused on the most plausible explanations.

Underthinking: Oversimplifying the Puzzle

On the other hand, underthinking occurs when you simplify the clues too much, dismissing details that could be significant. This can lead you to overlook vital information that would help you advance in the hunt. For example, if a clue references a "quiet place by the water," underthinking might lead you to assume it means any generic body of water, without considering whether the clue is referring to a specific lake, river, or stream with historical significance.

To avoid underthinking, take the time to consider each clue carefully and don't dismiss any detail too quickly. While not every detail may be critical, paying attention to even the seemingly small elements can help you stay on track and avoid missing out on the solution.

Avoiding red herrings is a critical skill in any treasure hunt, and Jon Collins-Black's treasure hunt is no exception. By learning to identify false leads and stay focused on genuine clues, you can improve your chances of success. Balancing your approach to the clues, avoiding both overthinking and underthinking, is essential to making steady progress. Red herrings are an inevitable part of the puzzle, but with the right strategies and a methodical approach, you can avoid getting distracted and stay on course to find the treasure. By honing these skills, you'll be better equipped to navigate the twists and turns of the hunt and uncover the hidden treasures waiting to be found.

Chapter 8: Advanced Puzzle Solving Techniques

Treasure hunts have evolved into an intricate and intellectually stimulating activity that demands advanced problem-solving techniques. The puzzles featured in Jon Collins-Black's treasure hunts, in particular, require a combination of diverse skills such as cryptography, the interpretation of visual and symbolic clues, and leveraging cutting-edge technology. As a treasure hunter, you must be adept at using all of these tools to decode clues, recognize patterns, and piece together hidden messages that will lead you to the treasure. In this chapter, we will delve into advanced techniques that can help you succeed in modern treasure hunts, from cracking ciphers to utilizing modern technology like GPS, drones, and online databases.

Cryptography and Ciphers: Unlocking Hidden Codes

Cryptography—the science of encoding and decoding messages—is one of the oldest and most effective methods for hiding information. Many treasure hunts, including Collins-Black's, employ cryptographic puzzles to hide the true meaning of clues or directions. Understanding the mechanics of various ciphers and how to crack them is essential for any serious treasure hunter.

Common Ciphers and How to Decipher Them

1. **Caesar Cipher:** Named after Julius Caesar, who used this cipher to encrypt his communications, the Caesar cipher is one of the simplest types of cryptography. In a Caesar cipher, each letter in the alphabet is shifted by a certain number of places. For example, if you shift the letter "A" by three places, it becomes "D," "B" becomes "E," and so on. To break a Caesar cipher, one needs to determine the shift number and apply it in reverse. Often, trial and error is required, but frequency analysis can help identify common letters like "E" or "T" in English text. A clue hidden

using this cipher could lead you to geographic coordinates or provide vital information about the treasure's location.

2. **Substitution Cipher:** Unlike the Caesar cipher, where all letters are shifted uniformly, a substitution cipher uses a random correspondence between letters in the plaintext and letters in the cipher text. Each letter in the original message is replaced by another letter from a different alphabet. The most famous example of a substitution cipher is the Zodiac Killer's cipher, which remained unsolved for decades. To solve a substitution cipher, one approach is to

use frequency analysis—since certain letters, like "E," "T," and "A," appear more frequently in English text, their cipher equivalents will likely correspond to these letters. Tools like frequency tables and online solvers can aid in cracking these types of codes.

3. **Vigenère Cipher:** The Vigenère cipher is a much more complex cipher than the Caesar cipher and is often used in modern treasure hunts. It involves a keyword that is repeated across the entire message. Each letter in the ciphertext is shifted according to the corresponding letter in the keyword. For instance, if the keyword

is "TREASURE" and the first letter of the message is "A," the letter is shifted by the position of "T" in the alphabet (the 20th letter). This cipher is more difficult to break because the shifts are not uniform. However, if you can determine the keyword, decoding the message becomes much easier. If you suspect that a Vigenère cipher is used, tools such as the Kasiski Examination method or online cipher decoders can help.

Transposition Cipher: In a transposition cipher, the positions of letters are rearranged to hide the message, rather than replacing letters with other characters. One simple method of transposition is to write the message in rows and then read it column by column. For example, the message "THIS IS A SECRET" can be written in a 4x4 grid:

T H I S

I S A S

E C R E

T S T

4. Reading the columns from top to bottom reveals the ciphered message "TIESTHASCRS." To crack this cipher, treasure hunters must look for the right grid dimensions or use trial-and-error to rearrange the letters and find meaningful phrases or coordinates.

Solving Cryptographic Clues in Treasure Hunts

When you come across a cryptographic clue in Collins-Black's treasure hunt, start by identifying the cipher. If the clue appears simple and involves a shift in the alphabet, it is likely a Caesar or Vigenère cipher. For more complex ciphers like transpositions, look for patterns in the arrangement of letters or symbols. Don't hesitate to use online cipher tools or collaborate with other treasure hunters on forums or websites, as crowd-sourced efforts can often yield faster results.

Visual and Symbolic Clues: What to Look For

In addition to text-based clues, many treasure hunts use visual and symbolic imagery to guide participants. These clues are often abstract, requiring a keen eye and an understanding of cultural and historical symbols. By recognizing the meanings behind these symbols and how they might relate to the treasure's location, hunters can unlock a new layer of the puzzle.

Types of Visual Clues

1. **Geometric Patterns:** Geometric shapes like circles, squares, triangles, and spirals often appear in treasure hunts and may have symbolic significance. For example, a circle might represent unity or eternity, while a triangle could symbolize a particular time or event. Often, these shapes are hidden within artwork, architecture, or landscapes, requiring

treasure hunters to look carefully for their placement and context. Understanding the meanings behind these shapes and patterns is essential for interpreting the clues correctly.

2. **Astronomical and Celestial Symbols:** Celestial symbols like stars, constellations, or the sun are frequently used in treasure hunts, especially when clues are tied to specific times of the year or locations on Earth. For example, a star may point to a particular direction, or the alignment of stars in a constellation might indicate a location. If the treasure hunt includes celestial references, consider researching the

star maps for the area or time period in question.

3. **Historical and Cultural Symbols:** Cultural artifacts or historical references often carry hidden meanings that provide clues to the treasure's location. Ancient symbols, such as those from Native American, European, or Asian cultures, can point to locations or dates significant to the puzzle. For example, a Celtic knot may reference a historical figure or location tied to Celtic culture. Similarly, symbols used in early Christian artwork could be tied to locations relevant to that era.

4. **Art and Architecture:** Treasure hunters should not overlook artwork and architectural features, as they can often conceal valuable clues. A famous example is the Mona Lisa, which has been speculated to contain hidden references to secret locations. In the context of Jon Collins-Black's treasure hunts, look for peculiar details in any accompanying images or maps that might point to significant locations or reveal hidden messages when analyzed closely.

Using Technology: GPS, Drones, and Online Databases

Modern technology offers a wealth of tools that can assist treasure hunters in solving puzzles more efficiently. GPS systems, drones, and online databases enable you to search large areas quickly, verify the accuracy of clues, and gather supplementary information to crack complex puzzles.

Using GPS and Mapping Tools

GPS technology allows you to pinpoint exact locations on Earth, which is particularly useful when a clue provides geographic coordinates or references specific landmarks. For example, if a clue in Collins-Black's treasure hunt provides a series of coordinates, you can use Google Maps or other mapping software to locate the point. Many treasure hunts also involve multiple locations that must be connected, and GPS technology can help you visualize these points on a map.

In addition to traditional GPS devices, GIS (Geographic Information Systems) software can offer even more detailed mapping capabilities, allowing you to layer multiple maps and datasets for deeper insights into a clue's potential meaning. GIS tools can help you analyze terrain, distance between locations, or even historical data to uncover hidden patterns.

Using Drones for Aerial Reconnaissance

Drones are becoming increasingly popular for treasure hunters who need to cover large or difficult-to-reach areas. Equipped with cameras and GPS, drones can fly over vast expanses of land and provide a bird's-eye view of the terrain, identifying landmarks or natural features that might otherwise be missed. In cases where the treasure is hidden in an inaccessible location, such as a remote cliff or dense forest, drones can offer a quicker and more efficient way to search these areas. Some drones are even equipped with thermal imaging, allowing hunters to detect heat signatures or other anomalies in the landscape.

Online Databases and Research Tools

Treasure hunts often require extensive research into historical documents, maps, and even obscure cultural references. Online databases are invaluable tools for this kind of research. Resources like JSTOR, the National Archives, and online museum collections provide access to historical documents, maps, and other primary sources that can offer crucial context for solving puzzles.

Crowdsourced platforms like Reddit, Discord, and specialized treasure-hunting websites also allow hunters to share their discoveries and pool resources. These platforms facilitate collaboration and can lead to the discovery of obscure information that could help you crack a particularly difficult clue.

Advanced puzzle-solving techniques such as cryptography, interpreting visual symbols, and utilizing modern technology are crucial for unlocking the hidden secrets of Jon Collins-Black's treasure hunt. By mastering the various ciphers, recognizing symbolic clues, and leveraging GPS, drones, and online databases, you significantly increase your chances of success. The key to solving any advanced treasure hunt is to combine your critical thinking skills with these powerful tools, and remember—collaboration and persistence are just as important as individual brilliance. Keep honing your puzzle-solving techniques, and with a little luck, the treasure could be within reach.

Chapter 9: The Hunt Is On: Where To Go Next

Now that you've acquired the necessary skills and knowledge for decoding the clues, understanding the puzzles, and using advanced techniques, the next critical step is putting your plan into action. Treasure hunting isn't just about solving riddles or cracking codes—it's about effectively organizing and executing a real-world expedition. In this chapter, we'll explore actionable steps for planning your next treasure hunt expedition, essential travel and preparation tips, and how to maximize your efficiency to cover more ground in less time.

Actionable Steps to Plan Your Next Expedition

Before setting out on a treasure hunt, careful planning is essential. An organized approach will increase your chances of success and ensure that you're prepared for any obstacles that might arise. Here are the key steps to planning your next treasure hunt expedition.

1. Gather Your Clues and Research Locations

Start by reviewing all the clues you've decoded so far. Break them down into smaller, more manageable parts, focusing on locations, symbols, numbers, and other key information that could point to a physical location. If the clues point to a geographic area, such as a particular state, park, or city, begin researching that region. Look for:

- **Landmarks:** Natural or man-made features that might be related to the clue. These could include mountains, rivers, buildings, or statues.
- **Historical Context:** Research the history of the area for any significant events or figures that might tie into the puzzle.
- **Cultural Significance:** Pay attention to any cultural references that might be connected to the location, as some puzzles incorporate symbolism tied to local customs or heritage.
- **Clue Correlation:** If you've decoded clues that point to specific coordinates or directions, start mapping them out. Use GPS or online mapping tools to

identify nearby landmarks and compare them against the clues.

This research phase can take time, but it's important to uncover as much context as possible before heading into the field.

2. Identify Key Locations and Prioritize

Based on your research, identify a list of potential treasure locations. These could be parks, towns, or specific geographic coordinates mentioned in the clues. Once you have your list, prioritize them in terms of feasibility and likelihood. Some locations may be more accessible than others, and certain clues may point more definitively toward a particular site.

- **Accessibility:** Consider how easy it will be to reach each location. Is it a remote mountain trail, a busy city center, or a historical landmark with easy access?
- **Terrain:** Take into account the physical terrain of each location. If the treasure is likely hidden in a mountainous region or dense forest, make sure to choose an accessible location where you can safely explore.
- **Clue Relevance:** Focus on locations that seem to align most closely with the clues you've decoded. Look for locations that have the necessary geographical and historical connections to the puzzle.

Once you've narrowed down your list, make a timeline for your expeditions and decide where to start.

3. Assess the Resources and Tools You'll Need

With your location in mind, you'll need to assess the equipment and resources necessary to carry out the hunt. Every treasure hunt may require different tools depending on the location and complexity of the clues.

Some tools and resources you may need include:

- **Mapping Tools:** GPS devices, online mapping software, or even old-fashioned paper maps. Being able to track your progress and mark important areas on a map is essential.

- **Survival Gear:** Depending on the environment, you may need camping gear, such as tents, food, water, and clothing for various weather conditions.
- **Safety Equipment:** First-aid kits, flashlights, and walkie-talkies can help ensure your safety during your search, especially in remote or difficult-to-reach areas.
- **Specialized Tools:** If the hunt involves physical clues like buried treasure or hidden artifacts, consider bringing metal detectors, shovels, or digging tools. Drones may also be

useful if you need to cover large areas quickly.

By preparing for the specific needs of your expedition, you ensure that you won't waste time searching for equipment or scrambling for resources in the field.

4. Set a Realistic Timeframe

Treasure hunts are often more complicated than they appear at first glance, and it's essential to set a realistic timeframe for your expedition. Estimate how long it will take to travel to the location, explore potential sites, and search for clues. If the area is large or the clues require a multi-day exploration, plan for several days of work.

Having a set timeframe can help you maintain focus and prevent burnout, ensuring that you don't get discouraged if the hunt takes longer than expected.

Travel and Preparation Tips for Treasure Hunters

Preparation for a treasure hunt involves not just physical tools but mental and logistical preparation as well. Whether you're traveling far from home or exploring a local area, the right planning can save you time, effort, and frustration.

1. Plan for Travel Logistics

- **Transportation:** If your treasure hunt location is far from home, plan your travel logistics well in advance. Book flights, rental cars, or other forms of transportation ahead of time. If traveling by car, consider the distance, possible stops along the way, and overnight stays.

- **Accommodations:** If the hunt requires an overnight stay, choose accommodations near your search area. This could include hotels, hostels, or even campgrounds if you're going to be exploring more rugged terrain. Be sure to check the availability of lodging before you leave.
- **Local Regulations:** Research the legal aspects of treasure hunting in the region you'll be visiting. Some areas may require permits for certain types of exploration, such as digging or using drones. Also, check if any local laws or ordinances affect your hunt.

2. Pack Smart: Bring Only What You Need

Packing efficiently is a critical skill for any treasure hunter. Consider the environment and potential challenges in the area you'll be exploring. Focus on lightweight, durable gear that won't slow you down, and ensure that you have everything you need without overloading yourself.

- **Clothing:** Pack appropriate clothing based on the weather. If you're hunting in a mountainous area, bring layers, waterproof gear, and sturdy hiking boots. For warmer climates, lightweight, breathable clothing and plenty of water are essential.
- **Communication Devices:** Always have a fully charged phone, and if

possible, bring a backup charger or a solar-powered charger.

Communication is key when treasure hunting, especially if you're exploring remote areas. In some locations, consider a satellite phone or two-way radio if mobile service is unreliable.

- **Navigation Tools:** Ensure that you have multiple navigation tools—GPS devices, paper maps, and a compass. GPS can be an excellent primary tool, but backup options are crucial in case of technical failure.

3. Local Expertise and Guides

If you're exploring unfamiliar territory, especially in remote or historically significant areas, consider hiring a local guide. Local guides can provide insights into the terrain, history, and potential hidden spots you might miss otherwise. They can also help navigate the local regulations, ensuring that your hunt stays within legal boundaries.

Sometimes, hiring a guide who is familiar with local folklore or hidden spots can give you an edge in solving puzzles. They may know of landmarks or geographic features that might not appear in official maps.

Maximizing Efficiency: How to Cover More Ground in Less Time

Treasure hunting can be physically demanding and time-consuming. Whether you're hunting in a large wilderness area or exploring a town with multiple potential clues, it's essential to make the most of your time. Here are a few strategies for maximizing efficiency and covering more ground without missing key details.

1. Break Down Your Search Area

Start by dividing your search area into smaller, more manageable sections. For example, if the treasure clues point to a large park, split the park into quadrants and focus on one quadrant at a time. This strategy can help you systematically eliminate areas where the treasure is not located, saving time and energy in the long run.

2. Work in Teams

If possible, gather a group of people to help with the search. A team can cover much more ground in less time and provide diverse perspectives on interpreting the clues. Divide the group into teams that tackle different sections of the area, and assign each team specific roles. Some may focus on deciphering clues, while others can physically search locations or use GPS tools.

3. Use Technology to Streamline Search Efforts

Incorporate technology such as drones or high-resolution satellite imagery to scan large areas quickly. Drones can cover vast expanses of land in a short amount of time, and with thermal imaging, they can help you spot anomalies in the terrain or detect heat sources that may indicate recent activity.

4. Track and Log Your Progress

As you search, document your findings, no matter how small. Record where you’ve been, what clues you've discovered, and any anomalies or notable landmarks that may lead to the treasure. Having a record of your progress can help you avoid retracing your steps and allow you to spot patterns that you might have missed in the moment.

Treasure hunting is as much about meticulous planning as it is about the thrill of discovery. By following actionable steps to prepare, plan, and execute your hunt, you ensure that you're ready for any challenges that come your way. With the right tools, strategies, and mindset, you'll be able to maximize your efficiency, stay focused, and increase your chances of uncovering the treasure—whether it's a literal chest filled with gold or a figurative prize waiting to be found.

Chapter 10: What to Do After Finding a Chest

The moment you've been waiting for has finally arrived—the treasure chest is in your hands. After weeks or months of decoding clues, strategizing expeditions, and navigating various obstacles, you've uncovered the hidden prize. But the journey doesn't end when you find the chest. In fact, this is just the beginning of a new set of considerations, from legal and ethical issues to preserving your discovery and deciding how to share the story of your adventure. In this chapter, we'll explore what to do after finding a chest, including the legal aspects of claiming your treasure, how to protect your discovery, and how to share your story responsibly.

Legal Considerations and Claiming Your Prize

Finding a treasure chest may feel like winning the lottery, but before you can truly enjoy your discovery, you need to understand the legal framework that governs treasure hunting. Laws surrounding ownership, property rights, and the protection of cultural heritage vary widely depending on the location and nature of the treasure, so it's essential to proceed cautiously and follow the proper procedures.

1. Understand Local Laws and Regulations

The first step in handling your discovery is understanding the laws in the area where you found the chest. Different countries, states, and even cities have varying regulations regarding treasure hunting and the ownership of found objects. Here are a few key legal aspects to consider:

- **Ownership of Found Property:** In many cases, the law determines who owns found property based on where it was discovered. For instance, if you find a chest on private land, the property owner may have rights to the treasure. Similarly, treasure found on public land could be considered government property, depending on local laws.

- **Treasure Trove Laws:** In some regions, treasure trove laws apply to valuable items discovered without a known owner, such as gold, silver, or rare artifacts. These laws may require you to report the discovery to authorities, who can then determine whether you have legal ownership of the find. Some laws mandate that treasures must be turned over to the government, with a reward or percentage offered to the finder.

- **Archaeological Finds:** If your chest contains historically significant or culturally valuable artifacts, you may be required to turn it over to a museum or government agency for preservation. In these cases, the chest and its contents may be considered part of the national heritage, and you may need to go through a formal process to claim it.

- **Federal vs. State Jurisdiction:** In some countries like the United States, federal law may supersede state law when it comes to discovering historical artifacts or treasure. For example, anything found on federal land (such as national parks, forests, or protected historical sites) often belongs to the government, and claiming it could result in legal penalties.

Before taking further action, it's crucial to contact a legal expert who specializes in property law or treasure hunting to help you navigate the regulations. They can ensure that you're following the proper procedures and not inadvertently breaking any laws.

2. Reporting Your Find

Once you're aware of the legal framework governing your find, the next step is reporting the discovery. If your treasure is significant or if you're unsure about the legal implications, consider contacting local authorities, archaeological experts, or a treasure hunting association. These entities can help you determine whether the chest should be reported to the government, a museum, or other relevant institutions.

For example, in the UK, treasure hunters are encouraged to report their finds to the Portable Antiquities Scheme, which helps identify and preserve items of historical significance. In the United States, the Archaeological Resources Protection Act (ARPA) regulates the discovery of valuable or culturally significant items on federal lands.

Reporting your find can also ensure that you're properly compensated for your efforts. In some jurisdictions, you may be entitled to a reward, a percentage of the treasure's value, or even the full ownership, depending on the nature of the find and the applicable laws.

3. Verify the Value and Authenticity

Before making any public announcements or claiming ownership of your treasure, it's essential to verify its authenticity and value. Take your find to an expert or appraiser specializing in rare artifacts or historical objects. Having the chest and its contents professionally authenticated will help establish its true worth, and it can also be helpful in any legal disputes over ownership.

In addition to verifying the physical value of the treasure, it's important to determine whether the chest's contents are of historical or cultural significance. Items of historical importance are often subject to different laws than purely valuable objects, and they may require special handling or reporting procedures.

Protecting Your Discovery

After finding a treasure chest, one of the most important steps is ensuring that your discovery remains safe—both physically and legally. Here's how to protect your find:

1. Secure the Chest

Your first priority should be ensuring that the chest itself is properly protected. Treasures often attract attention, and the last thing you want is for your find to be stolen or tampered with. Consider the following precautions:

- **Store It in a Secure Location:** If you're not yet sure what to do with your chest, keep it in a secure, locked location, such as a safe deposit box at a bank, a secure storage facility, or a personal safe. If the chest contains valuable or sensitive items, don't leave it in an easily accessible place in your home.

- **Avoid Publicizing the Find:** While it might be tempting to share your discovery with the world, doing so could put your find at risk. The more people who know about it, the more likely it is that others will attempt to claim it or take it from you. Keep your find under wraps until you've secured it and fully understood the legal implications.

- **Take Photos and Document Everything:** Before you move the chest or its contents, document everything with detailed photographs, notes, and a written description. This documentation will serve as evidence of the chest's discovery and its condition, should you need it in the future.

2. Consult Legal and Insurance Professionals

Once you've secured the chest, the next step is to consult with legal and insurance professionals. A lawyer specializing in treasure hunting laws can help you navigate the complexities of claiming ownership, while an insurance agent can assist you in securing proper coverage for your find.

In some cases, treasures can be worth millions of dollars. Protecting your discovery with comprehensive insurance will help you safeguard its value against theft, loss, or damage. An insurance policy specifically tailored to cover rare artifacts or valuable objects is advisable.

3. Consider Preservation Needs

If your chest contains rare or delicate items, such as ancient coins, manuscripts, or jewelry, you may need to take special steps to preserve its condition. Consult with a conservation expert to determine how best to preserve the contents of your find. For example, some artifacts may require specific temperature or humidity conditions to prevent deterioration, while others may need professional cleaning or restoration.

Sharing the Story: What to Expect After the Hunt

Once the legal and protective steps are in place, you may want to share the story of your discovery. After all, finding a treasure is an incredible achievement, and many treasure hunters take pride in sharing their experiences with others. However, sharing your discovery comes with its own set of considerations.

1. Media Attention and Publicity

If your find is significant, expect media outlets to take an interest. News organizations, blogs, and even television programs may want to cover your discovery, especially if the chest's contents are of historical importance or financial value.

Before going public, consult with a lawyer or public relations expert to help you manage media relations. They can advise you on what to say (or not say) in interviews, how to protect your privacy, and how to handle the influx of attention.

2. Ethical Considerations

While you may want to share your success with the world, it's important to consider the ethical implications of revealing the location of the chest. In some cases, exposing the location could result in the site being damaged by looters or treasure hunters who don't respect the historical significance of the discovery.

If the chest contains culturally important artifacts or items of historical significance, consider working with museums or academic institutions to ensure the discovery is handled with respect and preservation in mind. Some finders choose to donate valuable items to institutions that can properly care for them and display them for public education.

3. Financial Rewards

In addition to the personal satisfaction of uncovering a treasure, many hunters hope to receive financial compensation for their efforts. Depending on the nature of your find and the applicable laws, you may be entitled to a reward. This can include compensation from the government, museums, or private buyers who wish to acquire the treasure.

Consider your options carefully and weigh the pros and cons of selling the chest or its contents versus preserving it for future generations. Keep in mind that the market for rare and valuable objects fluctuates, and some treasures may appreciate in value over time.

Finding a treasure chest is an exciting and rewarding achievement, but the journey doesn't end when the chest is found. You must navigate legal considerations, protect your discovery, and decide how to share your story responsibly. By following the proper steps, from consulting experts to ensuring the chest's preservation, you can ensure that your treasure is handled with care and respect. Whether you choose to keep it for yourself, share it with the world, or donate it to a museum, your discovery will undoubtedly have a lasting impact—on your life and potentially on history.

Conclusion: The Spirit of Adventure

The treasure hunt is more than just about finding gold, rare artifacts, or riches hidden away in obscure locations. At its core, the pursuit of treasure is an embodiment of human curiosity, determination, and the quest for knowledge and discovery. The thrill of the hunt, the challenge of decoding clues, and the journey itself hold as much significance as the treasure. For modern treasure hunters, the true value lies not just in what is found, but in the spirit of adventure that drives the search. This conclusion explores why the journey matters as much as the treasure, how future adventurers can be encouraged, and what other hidden treasures—both literal and metaphorical—await us in the future.

Why the Journey Matters as Much as the Treasure

The idea of treasure hunting is rooted in the human desire to uncover something hidden, a universal appeal that transcends time and place. For many, the idea of finding a treasure is intoxicating, the notion that something of immense value—whether monetary, historical, or personal—is lying just beneath the surface, waiting to be discovered. Yet, while the end goal is an alluring part of the equation, it's the journey itself that often shapes the most profound experiences for treasure hunters.

Personal Growth and Problem-Solving

Every treasure hunt requires a deep engagement of the mind. From interpreting obscure clues to navigating geographical challenges, each step in the process demands creative thinking, perseverance, and a willingness to adapt. Treasure hunters develop skills in critical thinking, pattern recognition, and problem-solving that are applicable to various areas of life. This intellectual challenge becomes a form of mental exercise, pushing hunters to sharpen their reasoning abilities, analyze information from multiple angles, and continuously reassess their strategies.

In many ways, the hunt is as much about the process of learning as it is about the discovery of the treasure itself. Each puzzle, riddle, or challenge that needs to be solved becomes an opportunity for growth, learning new things about history, geography, art, and even human behavior. These aspects can make the experience more enriching than simply finding a chest filled with valuable items.

The Adventure of Exploration

Treasure hunting offers the unique opportunity to explore areas that might otherwise remain unnoticed or unexplored. Whether it's hiking through dense forests, diving into the depths of the ocean, or trekking across remote deserts, the treasure hunter is constantly engaging with the world in a way few others do. It's not just the treasure that calls out, but the landscapes, the environments, and the cultures that hunters encounter along the way.

In a world where many of us live more sedentary lifestyles, treasure hunting encourages a deep connection to the outdoors, and it fosters a sense of wonder and excitement. The journey to a hidden treasure often leads to breathtaking vistas, undiscovered historical sites, and a renewed appreciation for the natural world. This exploration can reignite a sense of adventure that many people forget they even have, reminding us of the vast and untamed parts of our planet that are waiting to be explored.

Shared Experiences and Connections

Treasure hunts are rarely solitary endeavors. Whether through online forums, treasure hunting groups, or partnerships with other hunters, many seekers share the journey together. The camaraderie that develops within these communities is one of the most fulfilling aspects of treasure hunting. These connections—often formed between strangers with a shared passion—can turn into long-lasting friendships.

The journey toward uncovering treasure is, in a way, a journey of connection. It brings people together from different walks of life, united by the pursuit of a common goal. It's not just about finding the treasure but also about forming bonds, sharing insights, and learning from one another. For many treasure hunters, the relationships they build along the way are as valuable as the treasures they seek.

Encouraging Future Adventurers

As we look toward the future, it's essential to encourage the next generation of adventurers to take up the mantle of treasure hunting and exploration. In a world increasingly dominated by digital screens and virtual experiences, the art of physical exploration is often overshadowed by more sedentary pastimes. Yet, the spirit of adventure—along with the tangible rewards that come from exploration—remains an irreplaceable part of the human experience.

Promoting Curiosity and Creativity

The first step in encouraging future treasure hunters is promoting curiosity and creativity. Treasure hunting is about more than just following a map or solving a riddle; it's about being able to think critically, consider alternative perspectives, and make connections between seemingly unrelated ideas. By fostering these skills in young people, we can ignite a passion for discovery that goes beyond the treasure hunt and extends into every aspect of their lives.

Education, both formal and informal, plays a key role in shaping how young minds approach challenges. Encouraging students to participate in problem-solving activities, engage with historical narratives, and explore local geography can be a gateway to the world of treasure hunting. Programs that encourage exploration, whether through clubs, competitions, or field trips, can help cultivate a spirit of adventure that motivates children to look for their own hidden treasures in the world around them.

Utilizing Technology and Online Resources

Today's technology opens up a wealth of opportunities for aspiring treasure hunters. Platforms like Reddit, Discord, and other online forums allow people from all corners of the globe to collaborate, share their discoveries, and even crowdsource information. The internet has made it possible for treasure hunters to learn from others, share clues, and connect with experts who can provide insights on treasure maps, ciphers, and historical research.

Future adventurers can benefit from the wealth of knowledge and resources available online. YouTube tutorials, treasure hunting blogs, and digital map services can help hunters navigate new terrains, decode complex clues, and connect with like-minded individuals. By embracing technology, the next generation of treasure hunters will have access to tools that their predecessors could only dream of.

Real-World Opportunities for Exploration

While virtual games and online puzzles are popular today, real-world treasure hunting offers a more tangible and immersive experience. Encouraging young adventurers to participate in activities like geocaching, local history tours, and outdoor exploration provides an accessible gateway into the world of treasure hunting. Many treasure hunts are organized in cities, national parks, and heritage sites, allowing aspiring hunters to test their skills and knowledge in real-world environments.

Incorporating aspects of treasure hunting into educational programs can also inspire young people to take their learning outside the classroom. For instance, history lessons could be supplemented with field trips to archaeological sites, where students can actively participate in the discovery and study of historical artifacts. This hands-on learning can instill a lifelong appreciation for exploration and problem-solving.

Looking Beyond: What Other Modern Treasures Await?

As we consider the future of treasure hunting, it's clear that there is still much to discover in our world. While many treasure hunters focus on hidden caches of gold, jewels, and ancient relics, modern treasures can take many forms—both material and metaphorical.

Technological and Environmental Treasures

In today's world, some of the most exciting treasures are hidden in the digital realm and the natural world. With the rise of virtual reality (VR), augmented reality (AR), and digital mapping technologies, new treasure hunts are emerging that blend the digital and physical worlds. These modern treasure hunts may involve virtual clues, interactive maps, or geospatial technology, offering an entirely new type of adventure for the tech-savvy adventurer.

Environmental treasures also represent an exciting frontier for modern explorers. As we continue to study ecosystems, ancient fossils, and uncharted regions, there are untold discoveries waiting to be made. Hidden natural wonders, new species, and ancient landscapes are all potential "treasures" for those brave enough to venture into the unknown. Scientific expeditions, environmental conservation projects, and geological explorations all represent modern equivalents of the treasure hunt, with significant implications for our understanding of the planet.

Intellectual Treasures

Beyond physical discoveries, intellectual treasures also await those who seek them. The process of unraveling mysteries, solving ancient riddles, and deciphering historical enigmas has the power to change our understanding of the past. Many of today's great minds are treasure hunters in their own right, uncovering the lost secrets of humanity through archaeological digs, historical research, and linguistic analysis.

Future treasure hunters may find themselves on quests to recover lost knowledge, decode cryptic messages from ancient civilizations, or unearth forgotten scientific theories that could alter the course of history. These intellectual treasures, while intangible, carry profound significance and promise to shape the future of knowledge.

Treasure hunting, at its essence, is about much more than simply uncovering material wealth. It's a journey of discovery, learning, and connection, one that fosters curiosity, problem-solving, and a love for exploration. While the treasure may be the goal, the journey is where the true rewards lie. As we encourage the next generation of adventurers to follow in the footsteps of past treasure hunters, we're not just passing on the tools for finding gold and jewels; we're passing on the spirit of adventure itself. And as the world continues to evolve, new treasures—both tangible and intellectual—await those who dare to seek them. The hunt is never truly over.

Made in the USA
Las Vegas, NV
13 December 2024